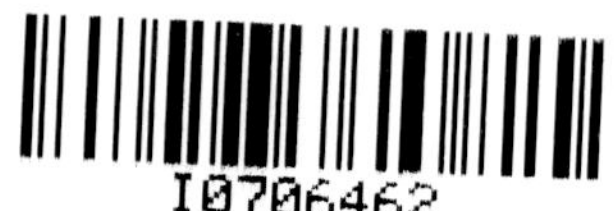

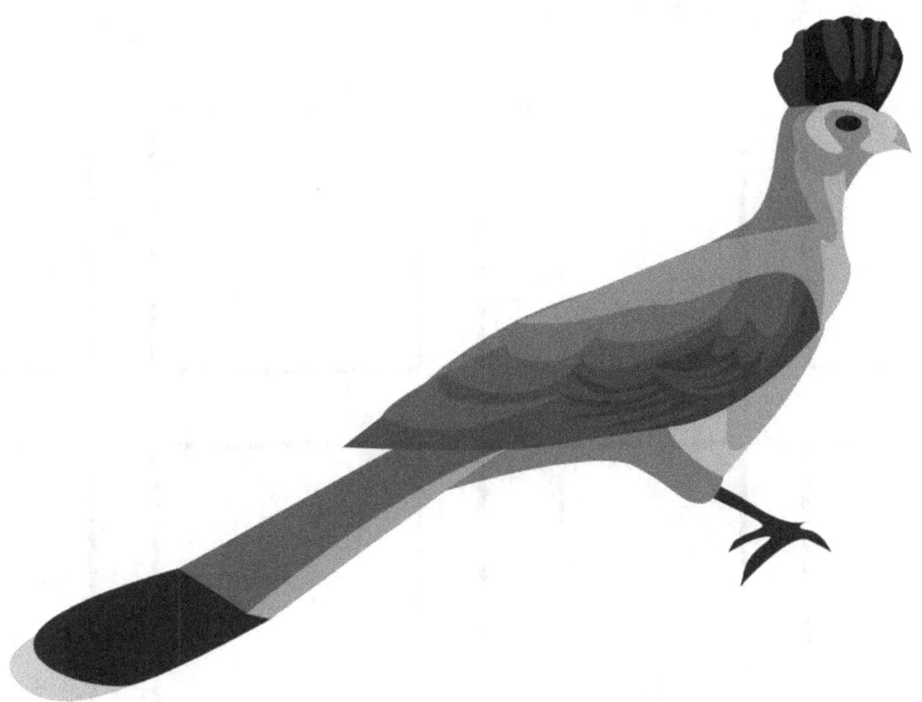

This Book Belongs To:

....

....

....

Coloring Test Page

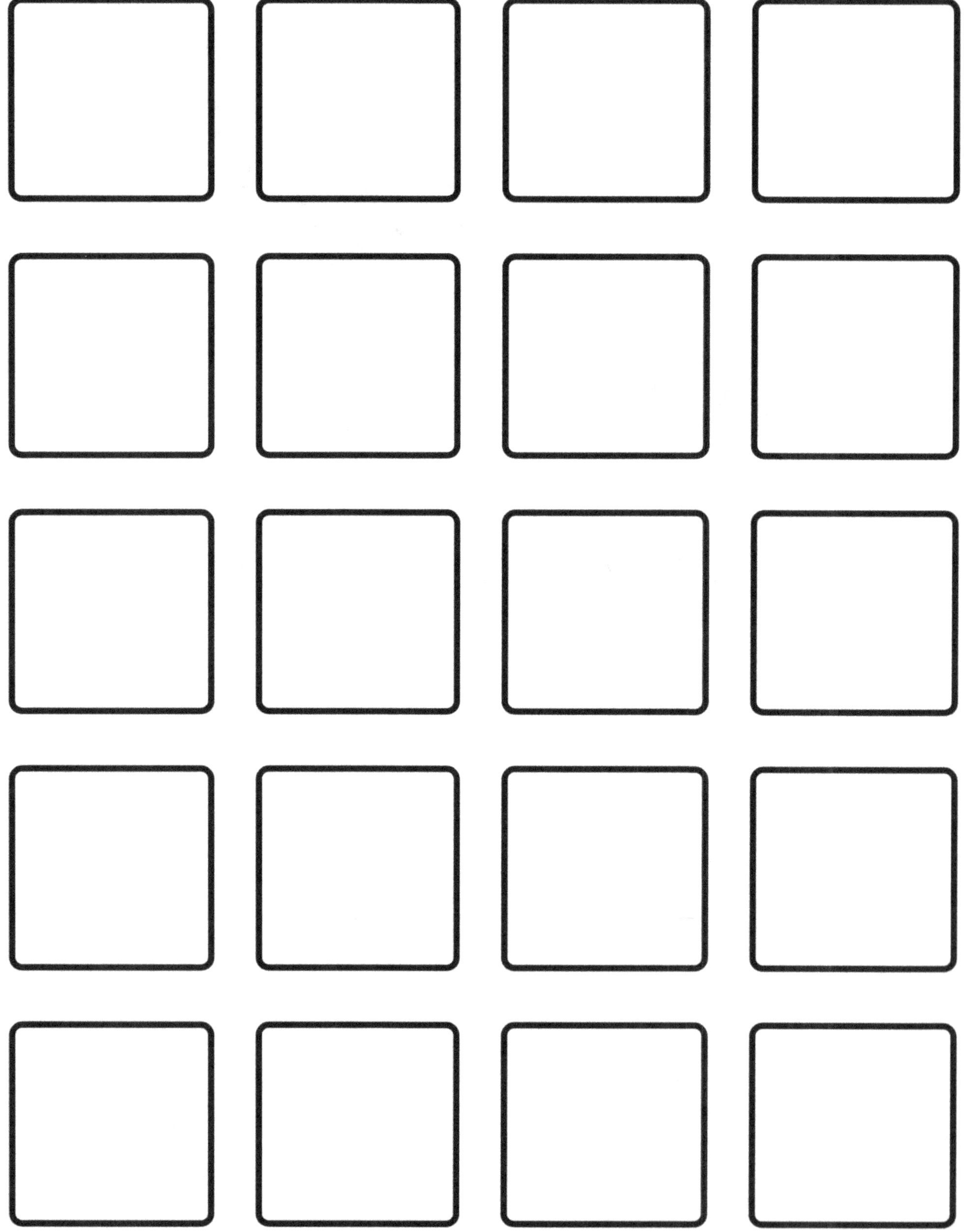

Coloring Test Page

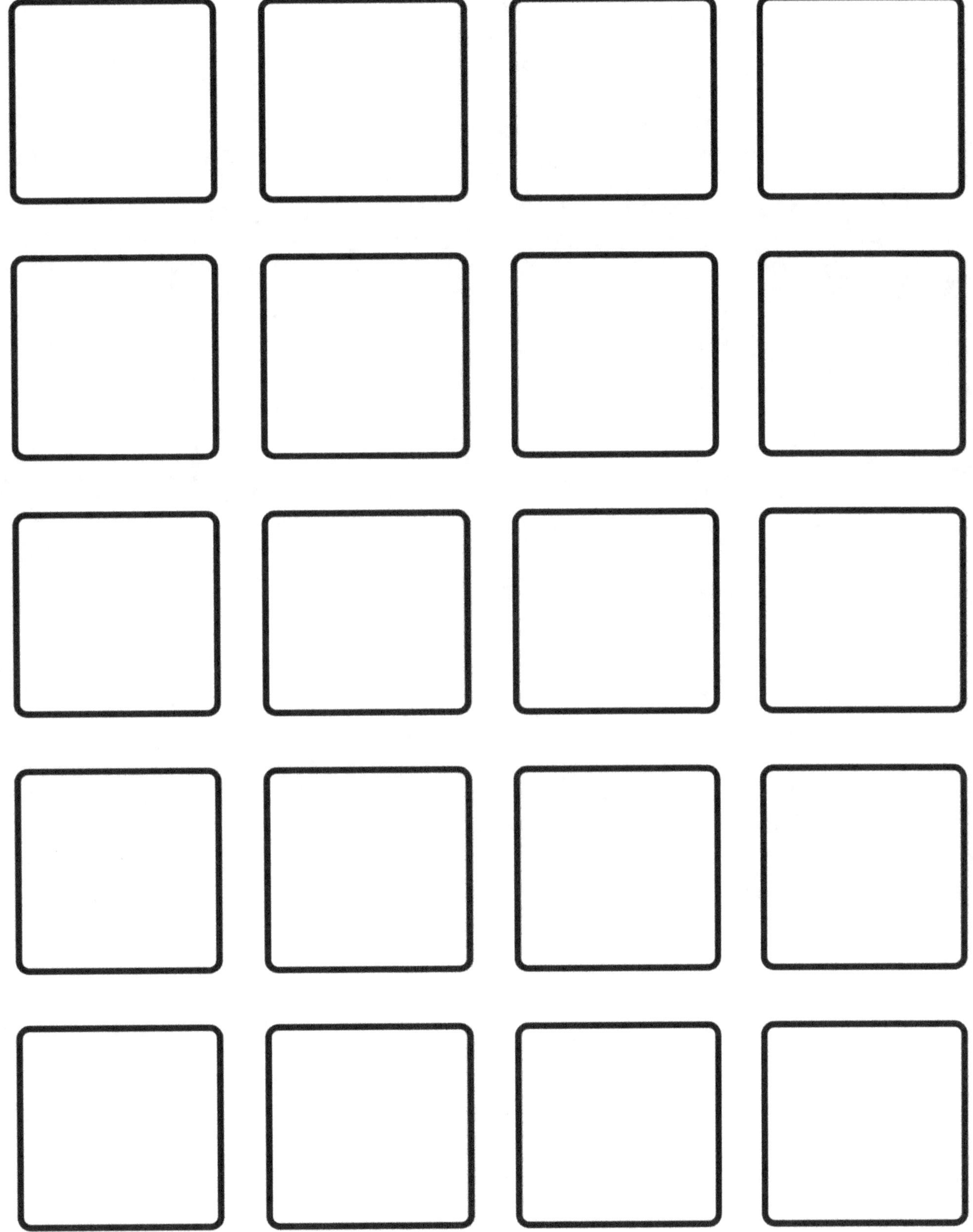

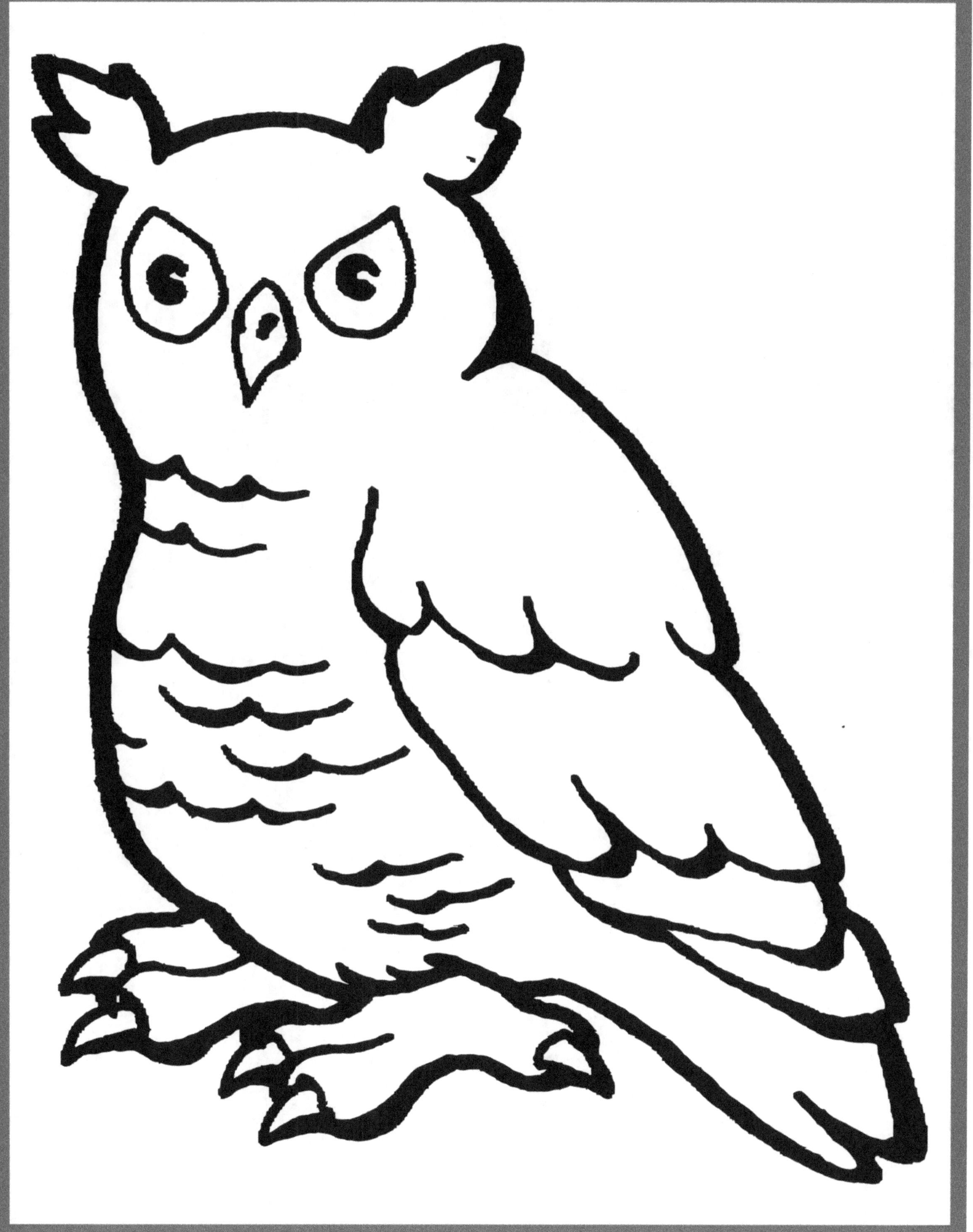

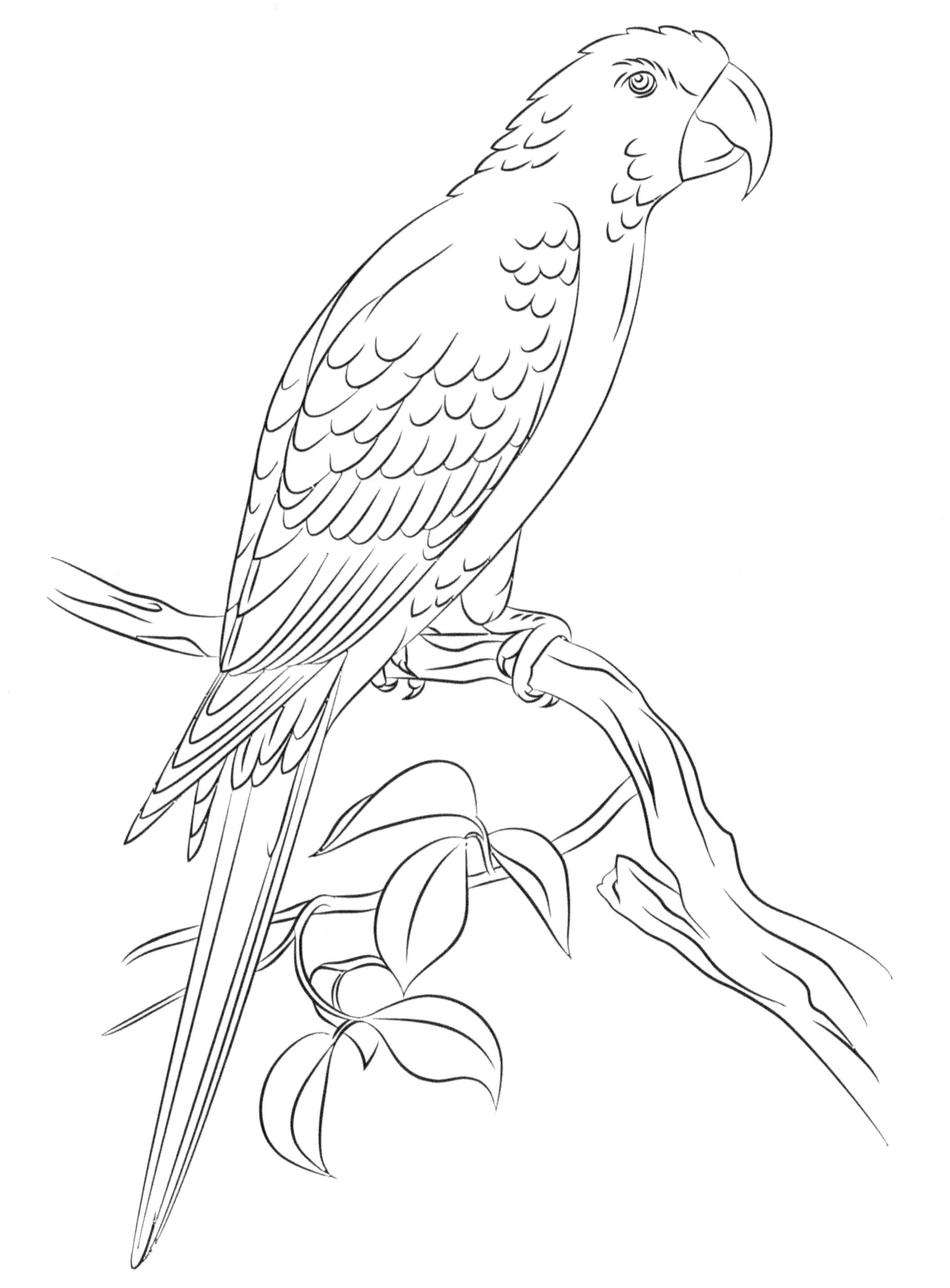

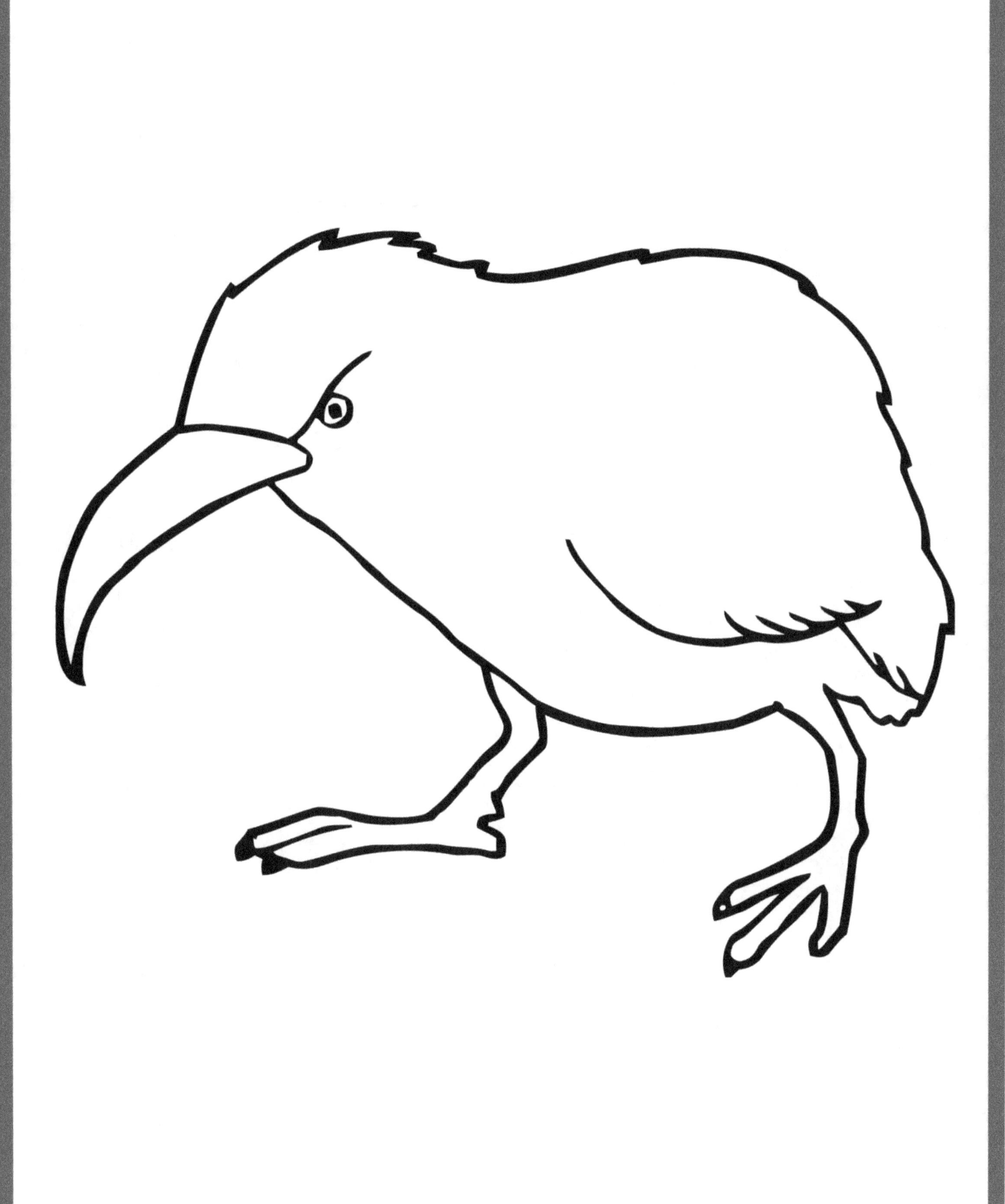

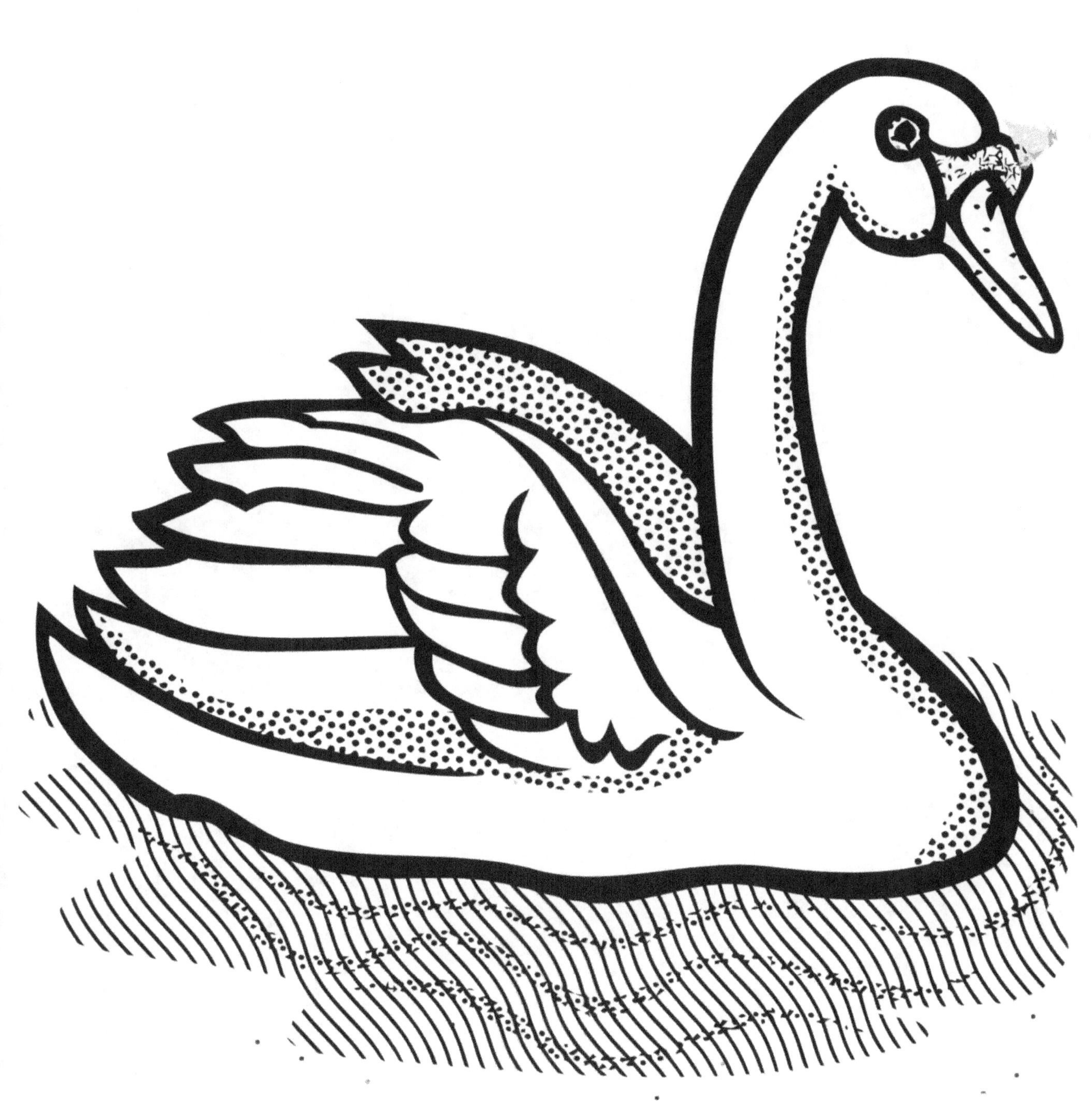

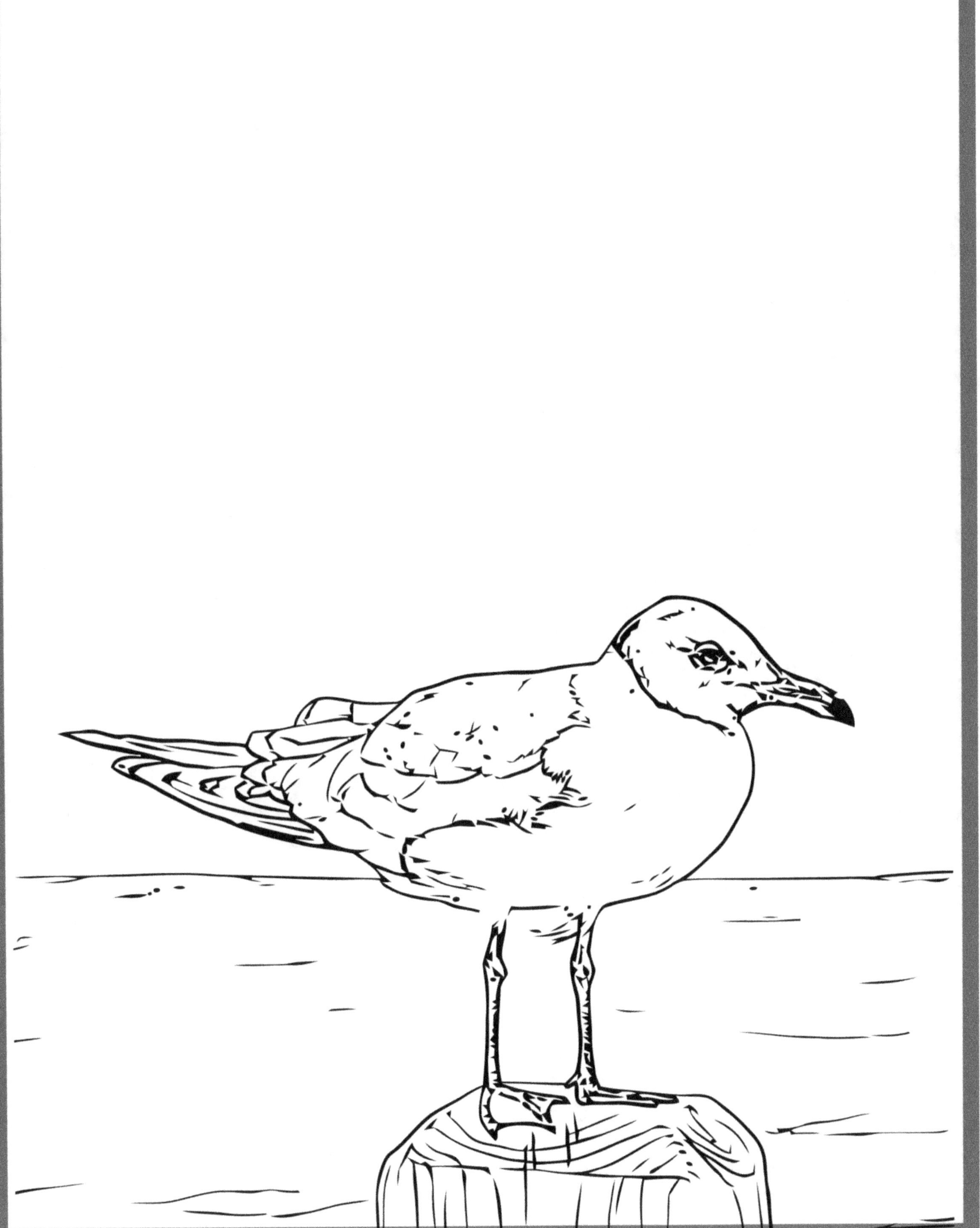

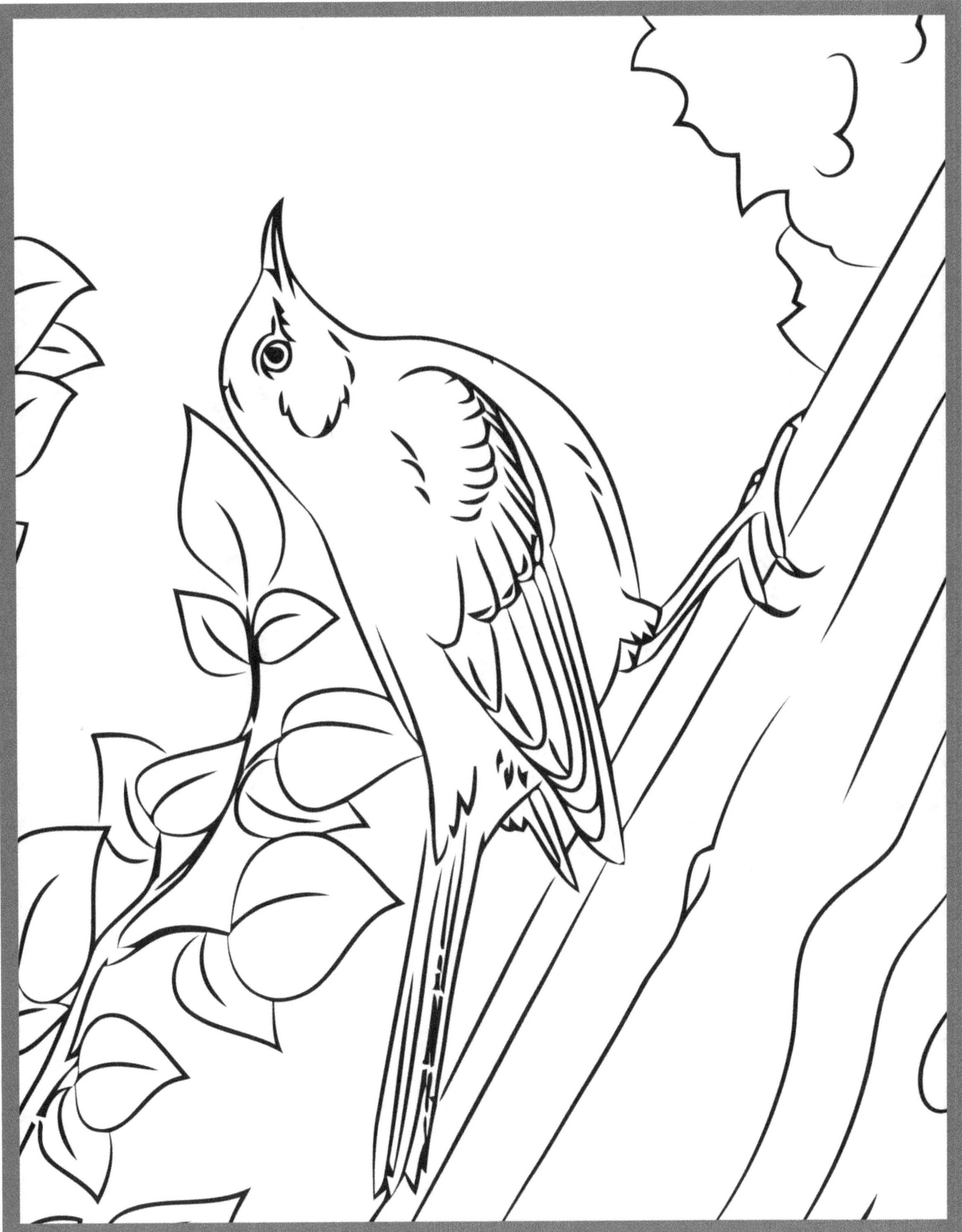

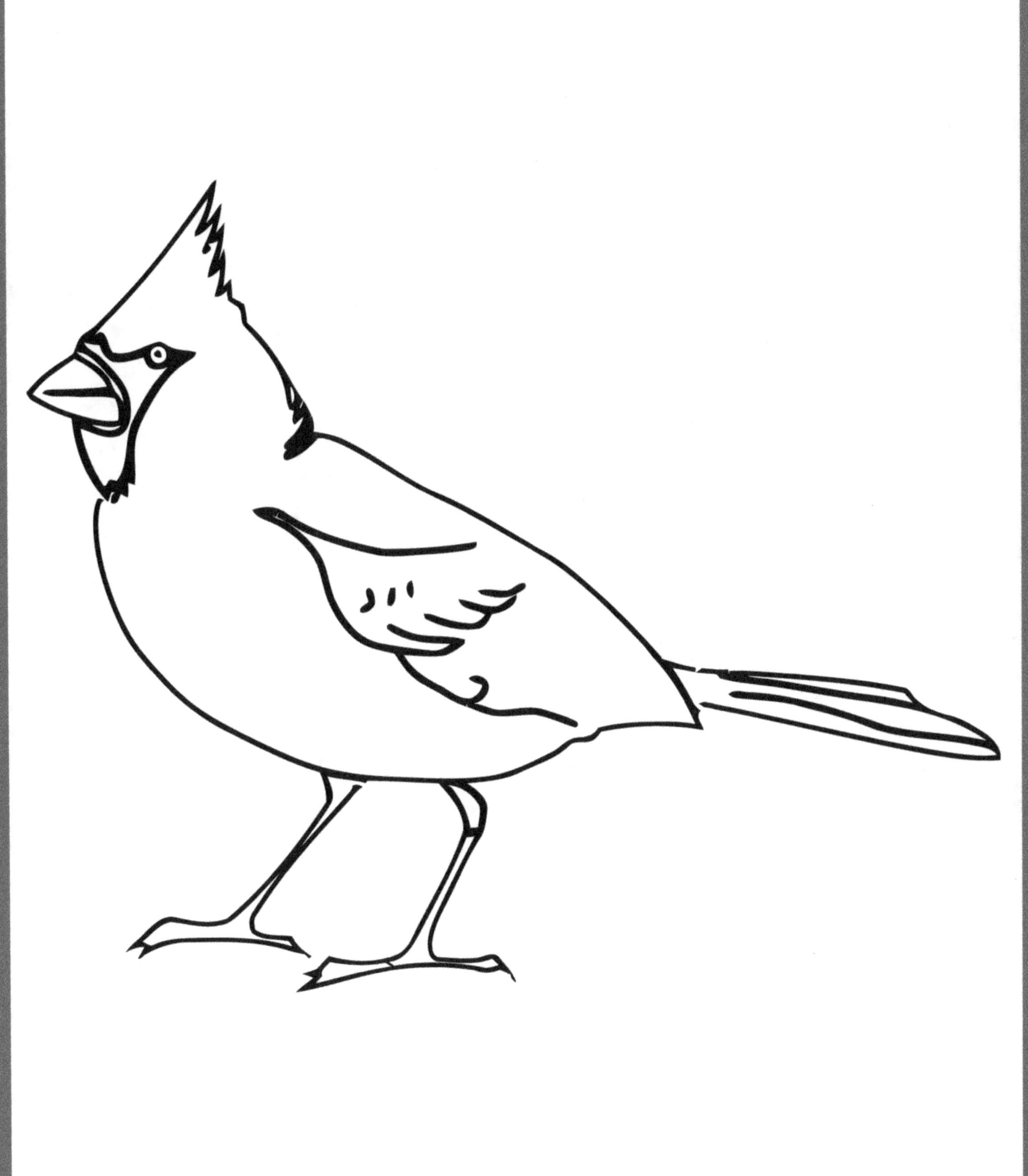

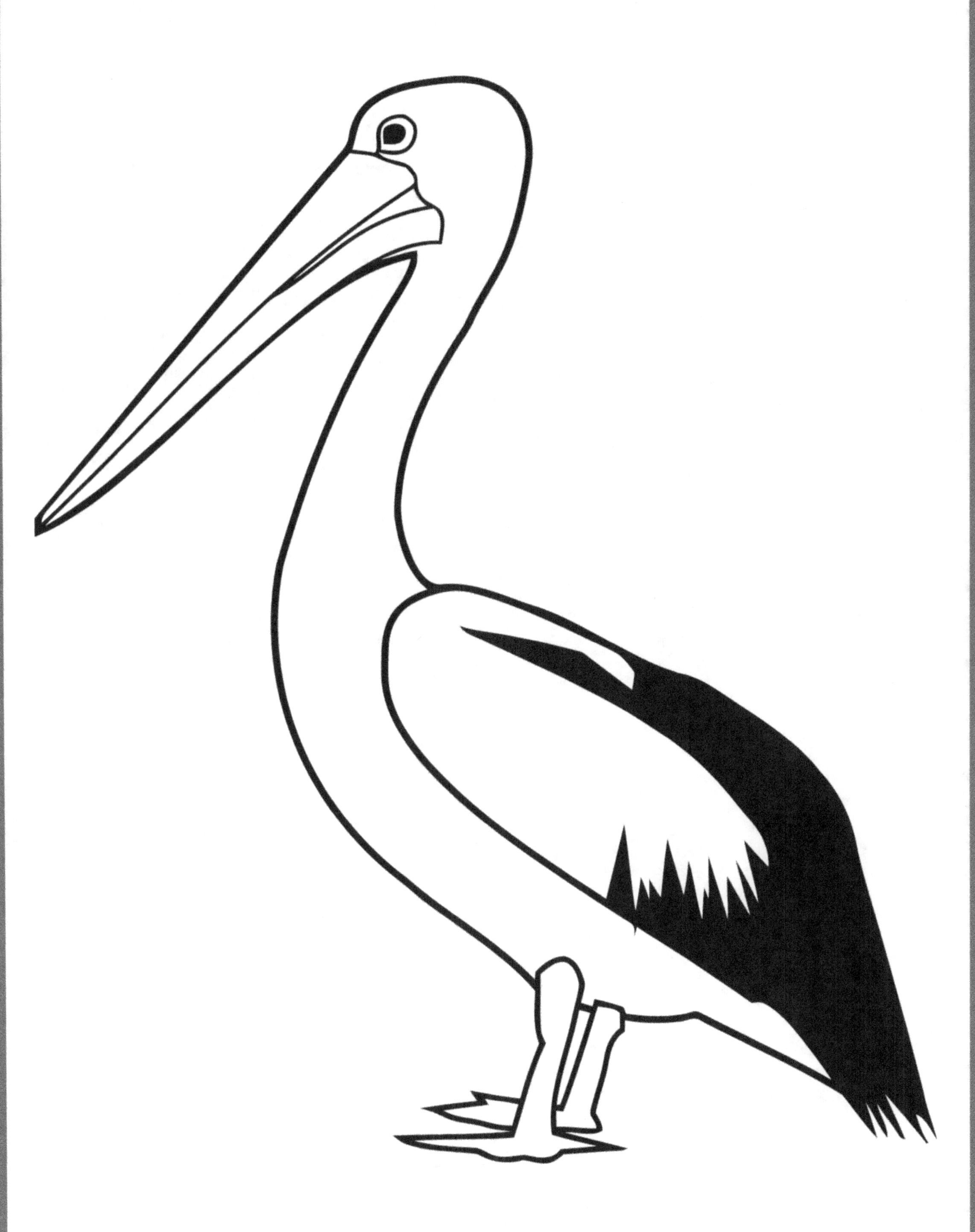

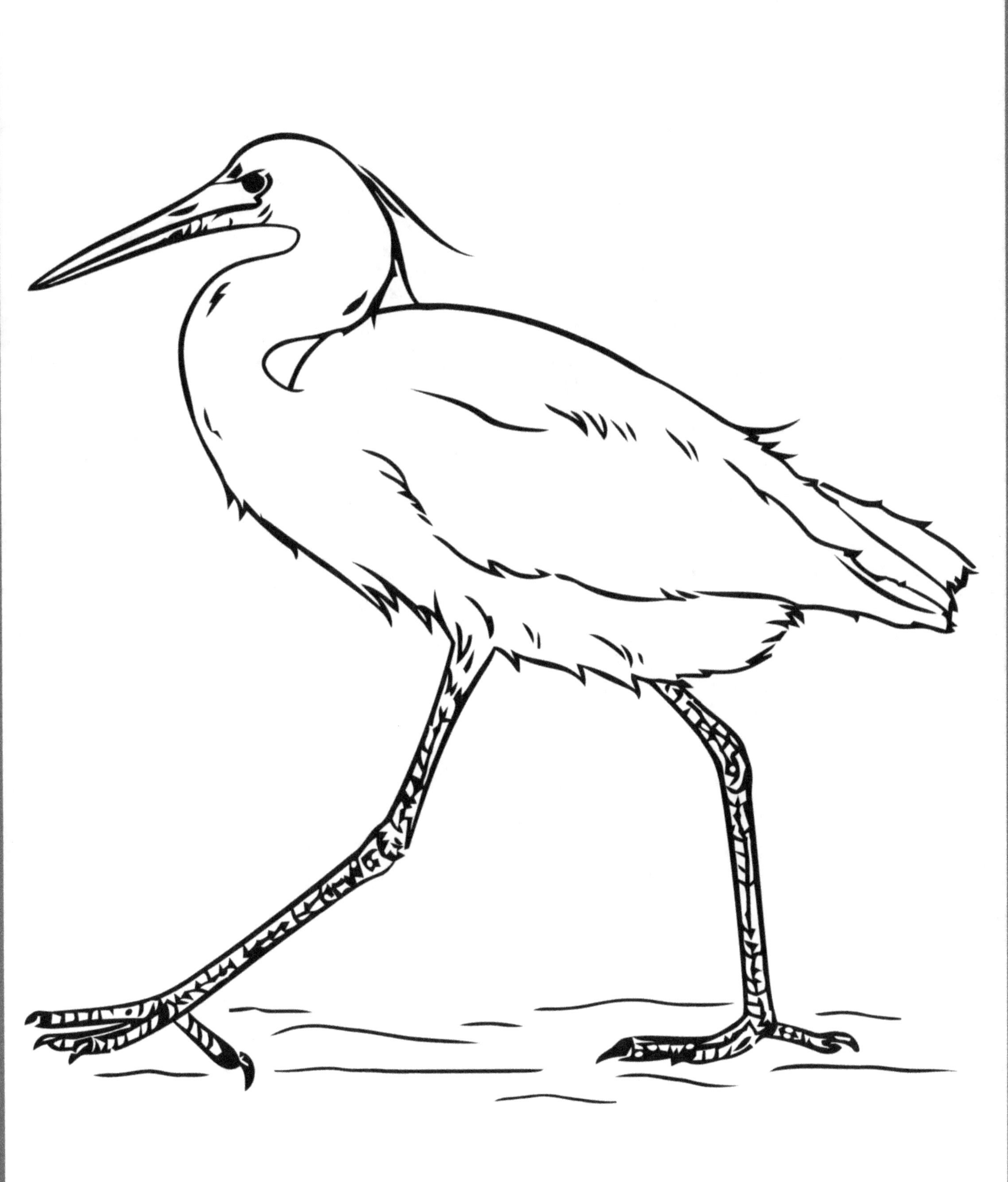

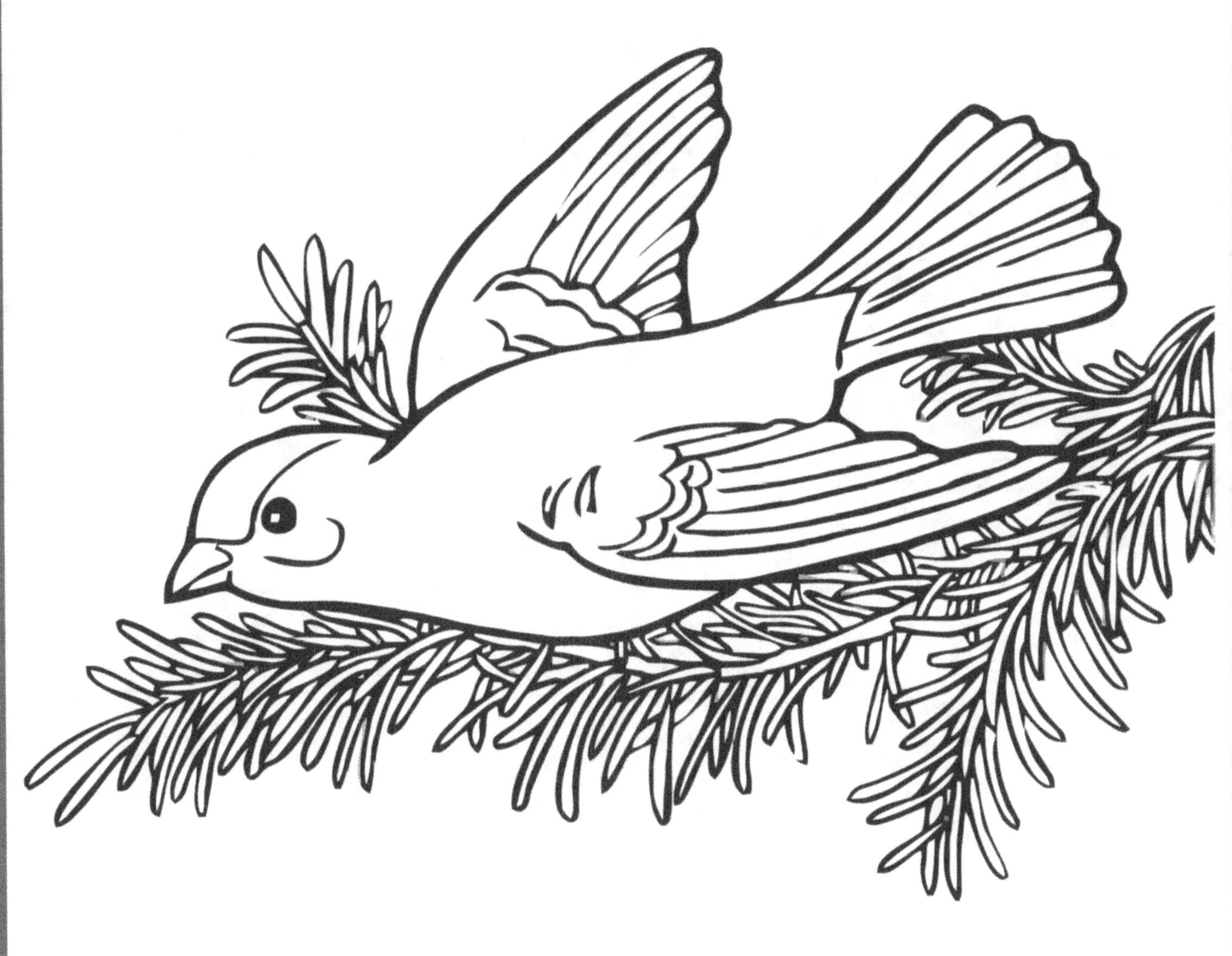

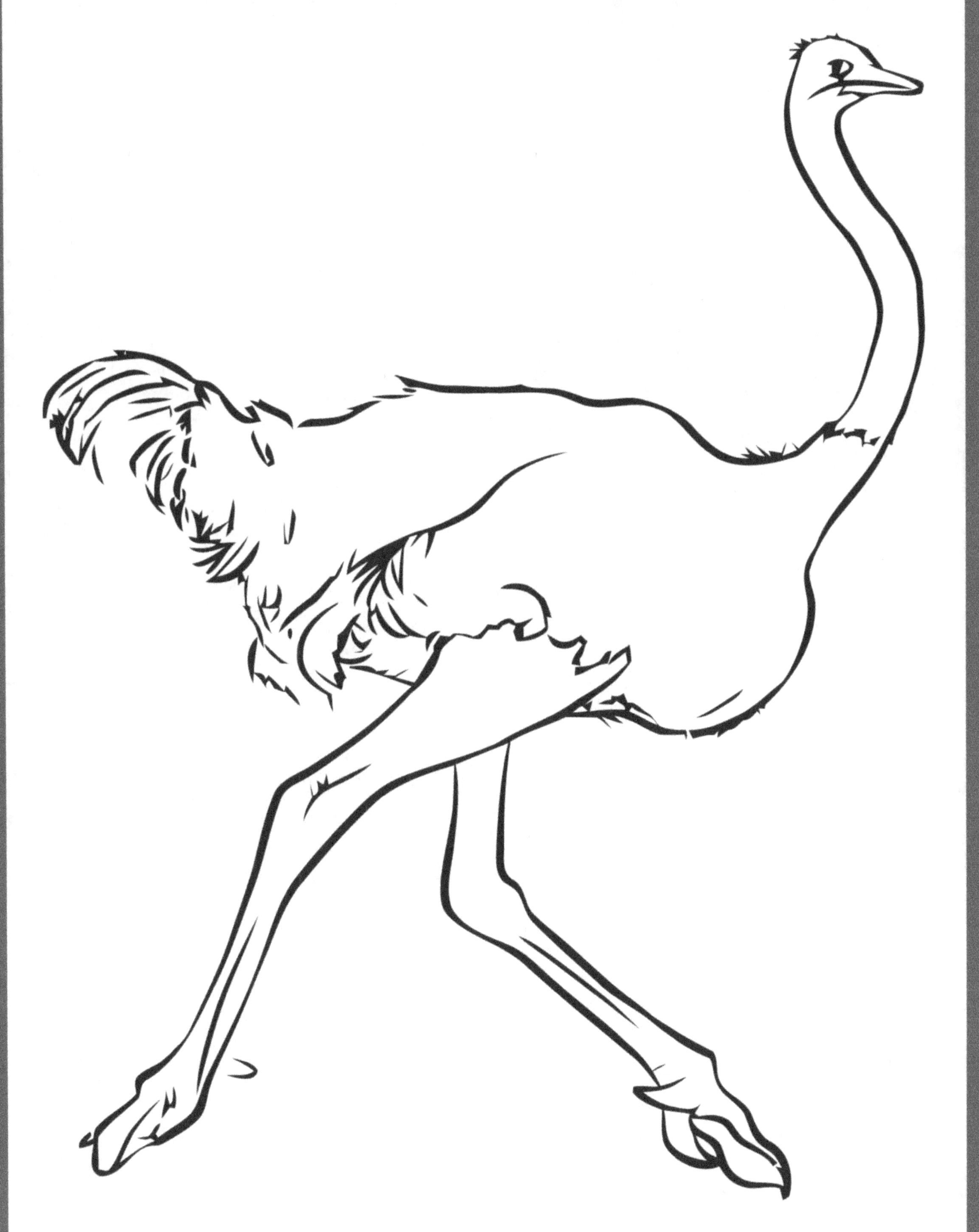

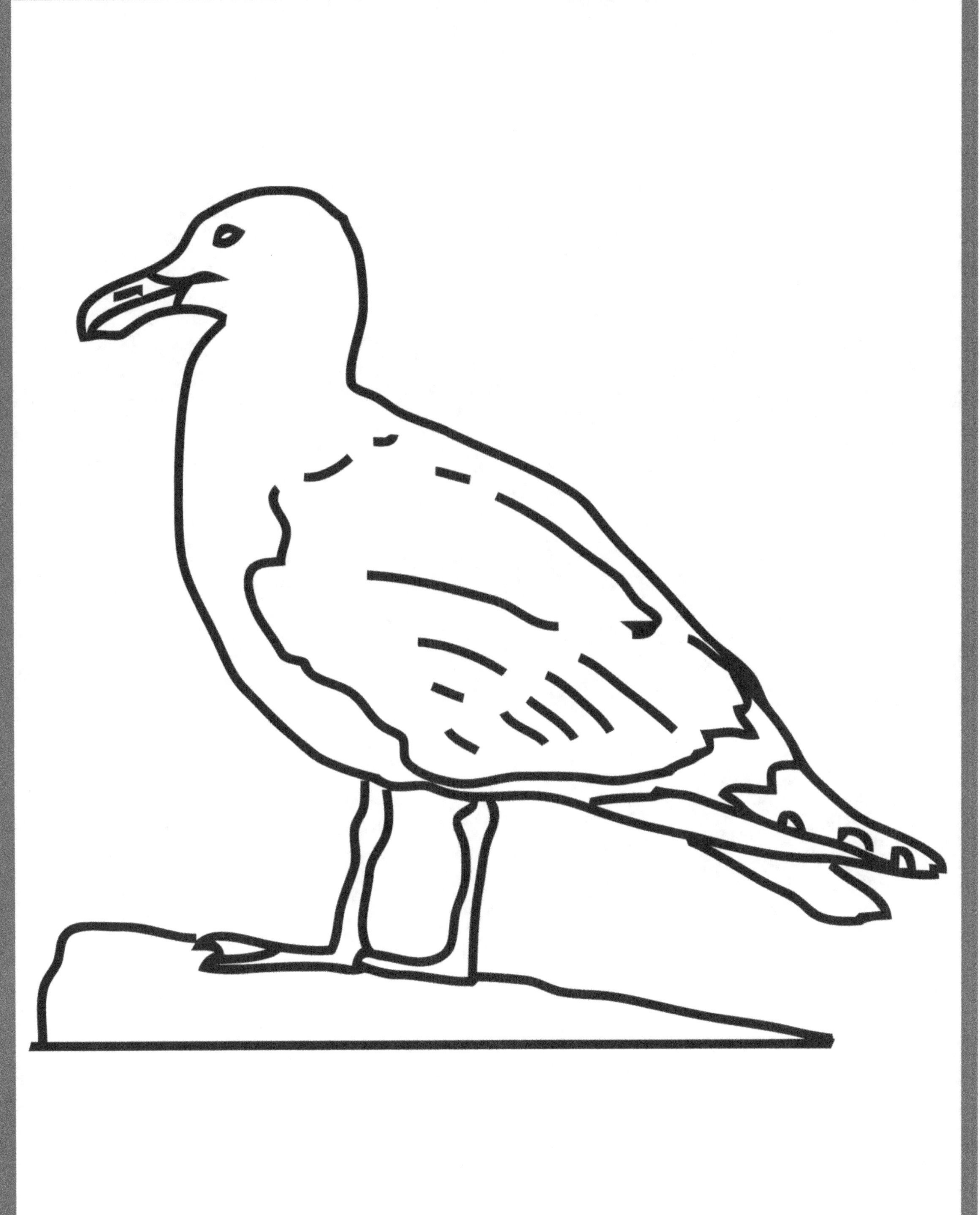

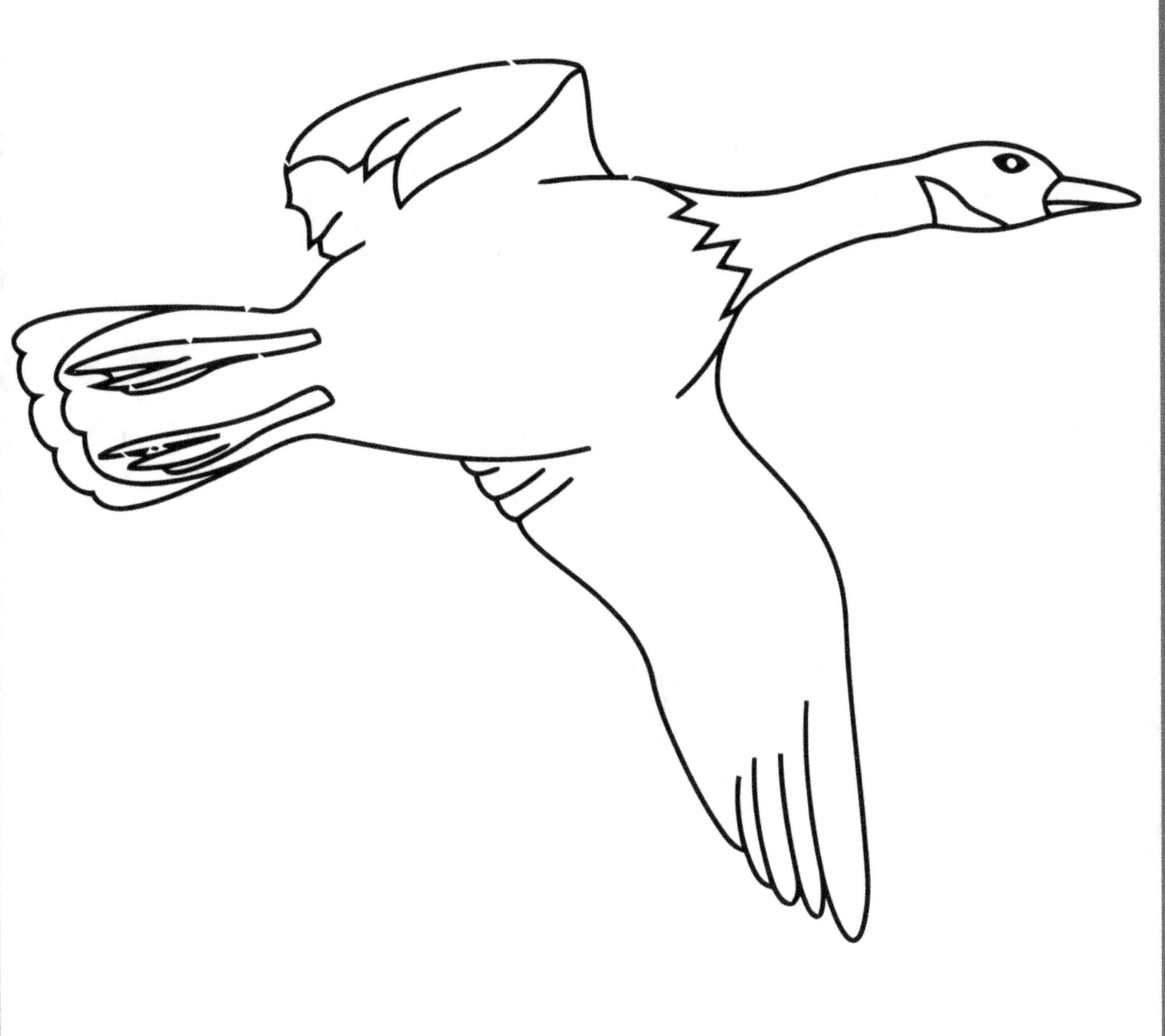

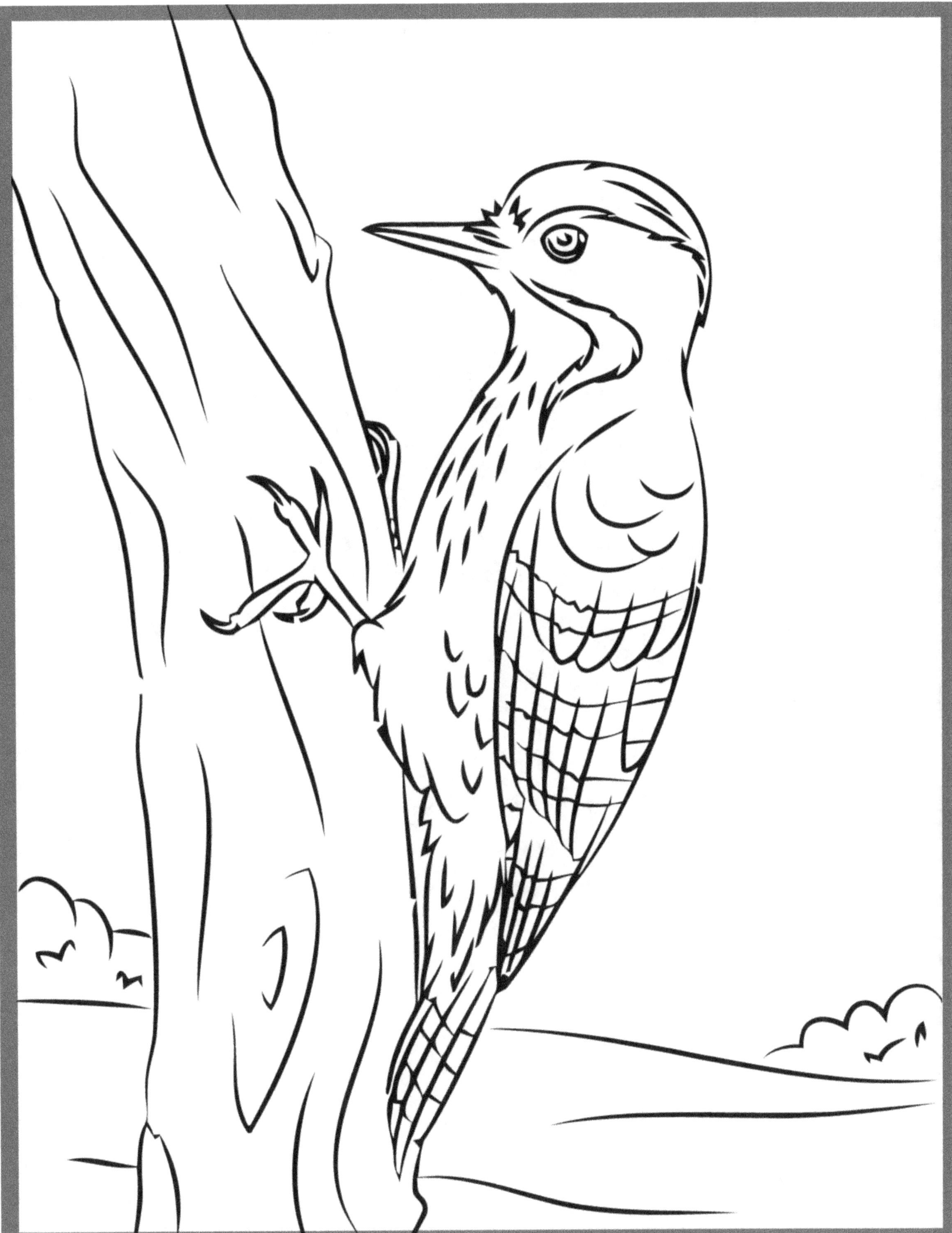

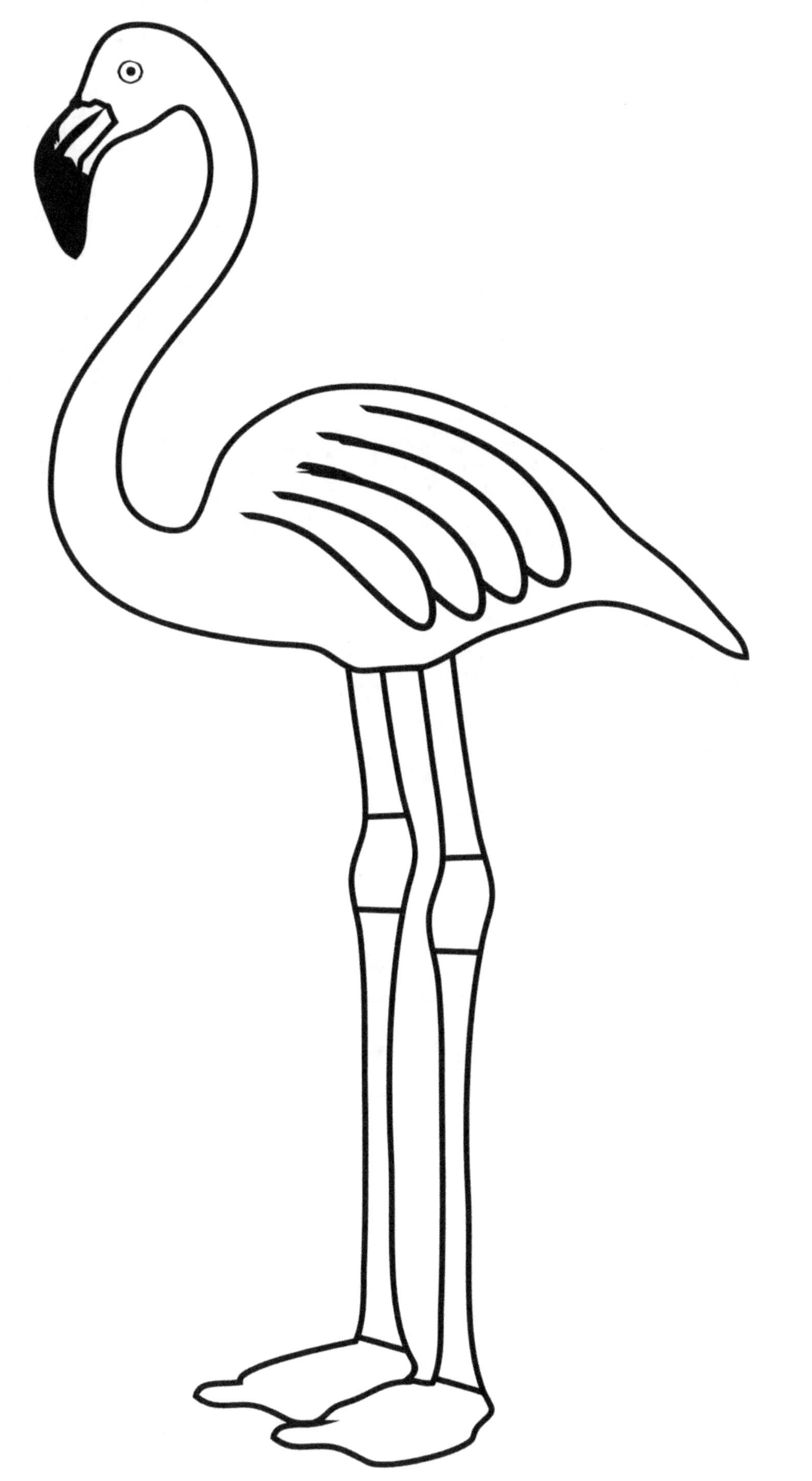

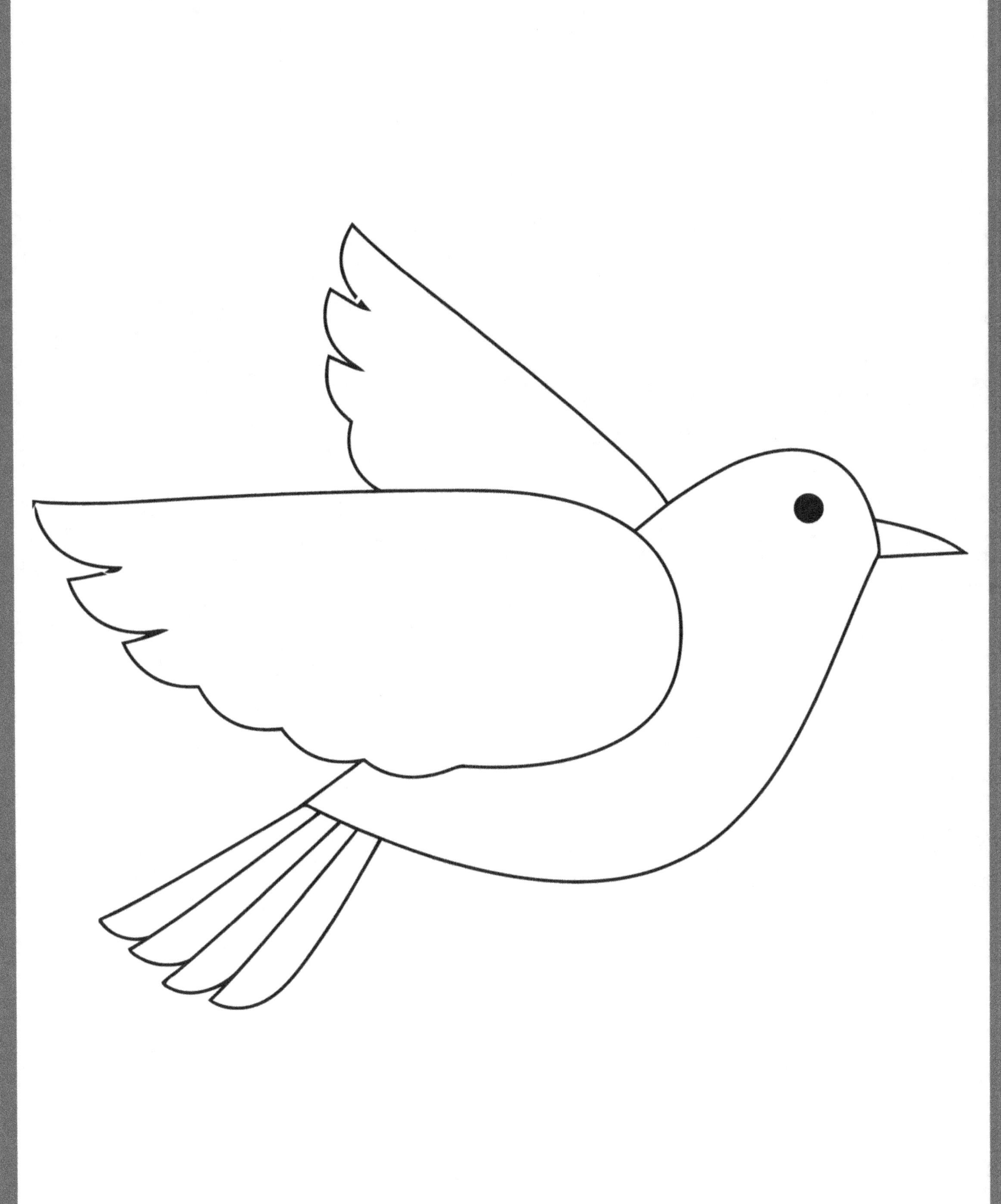

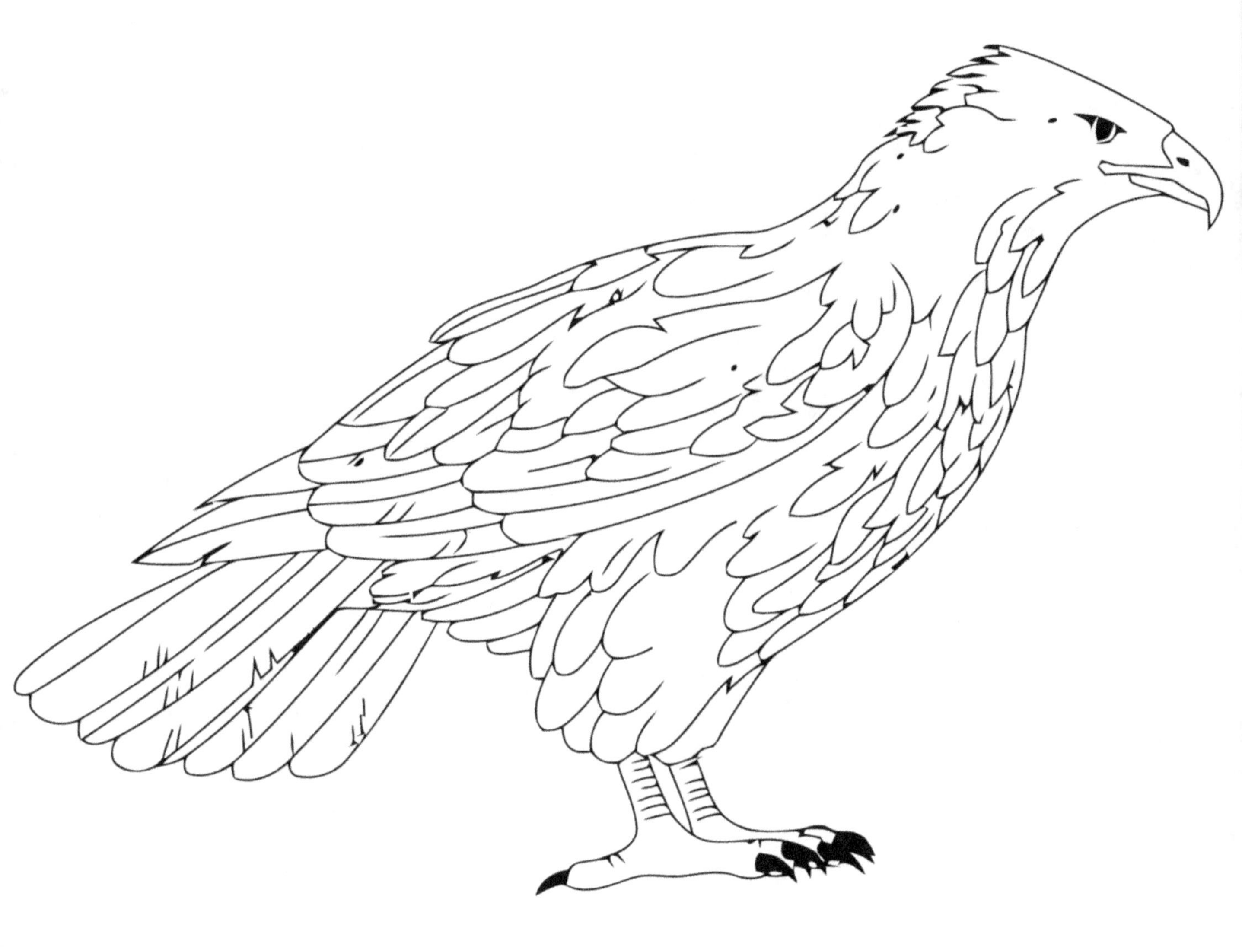

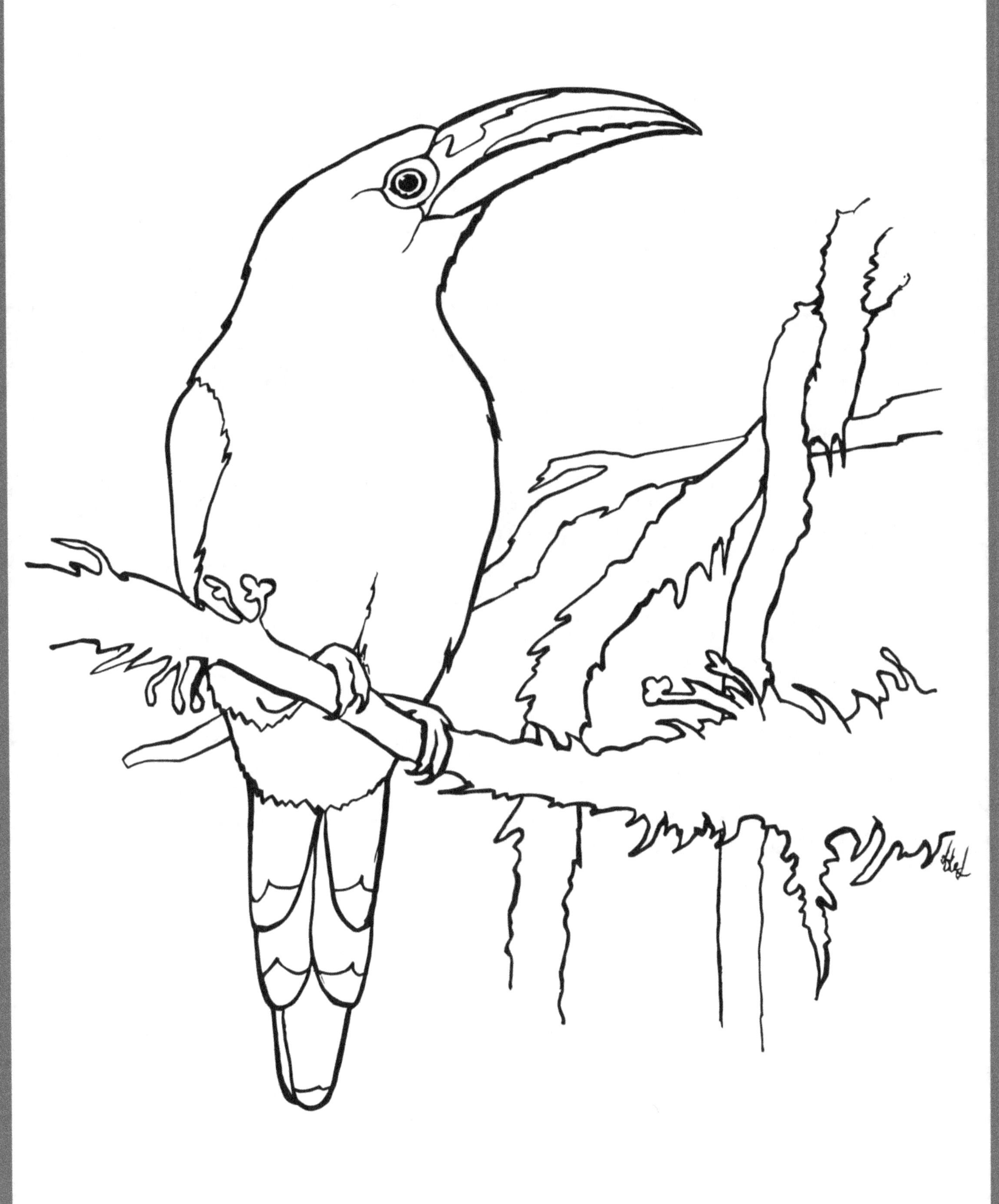

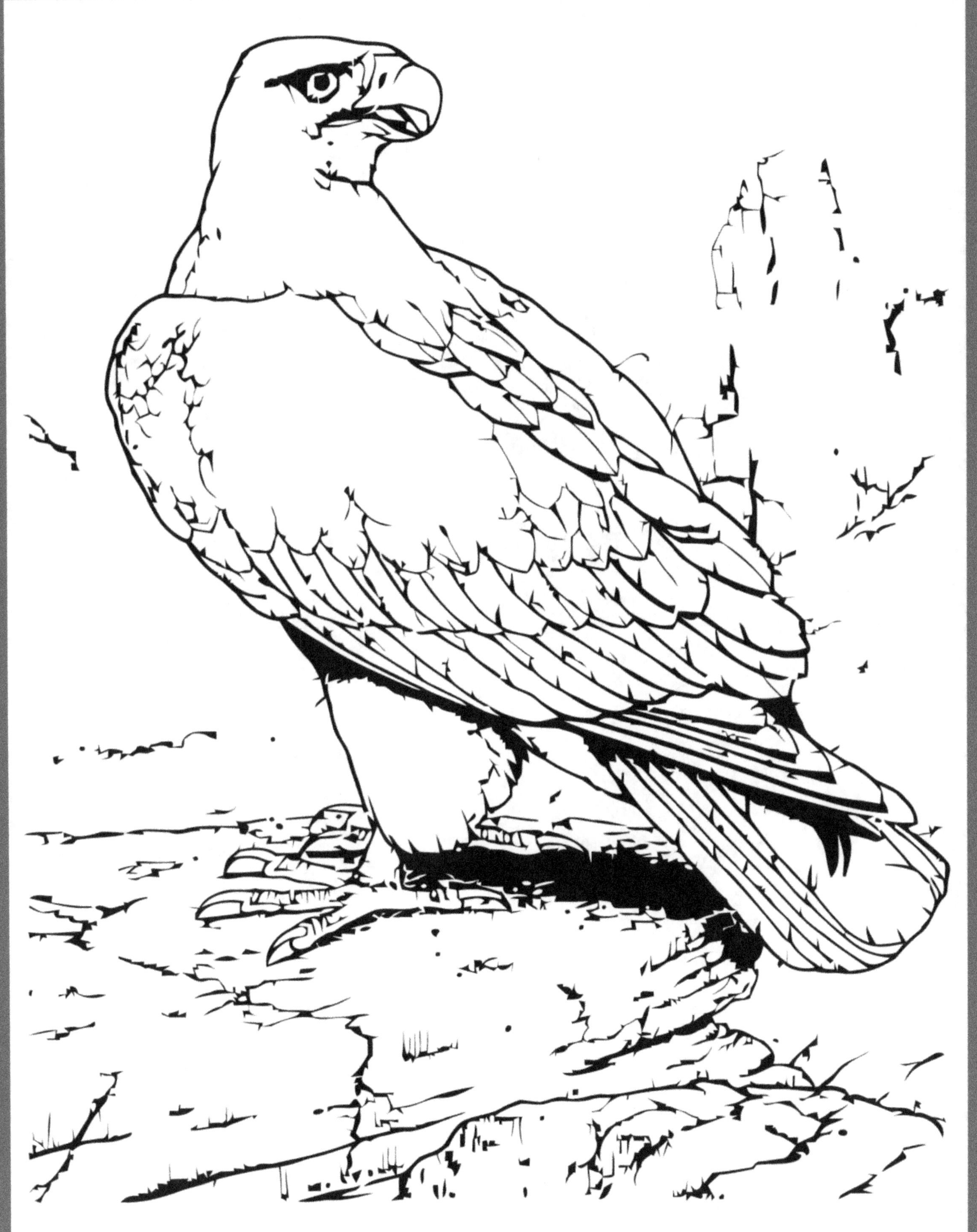

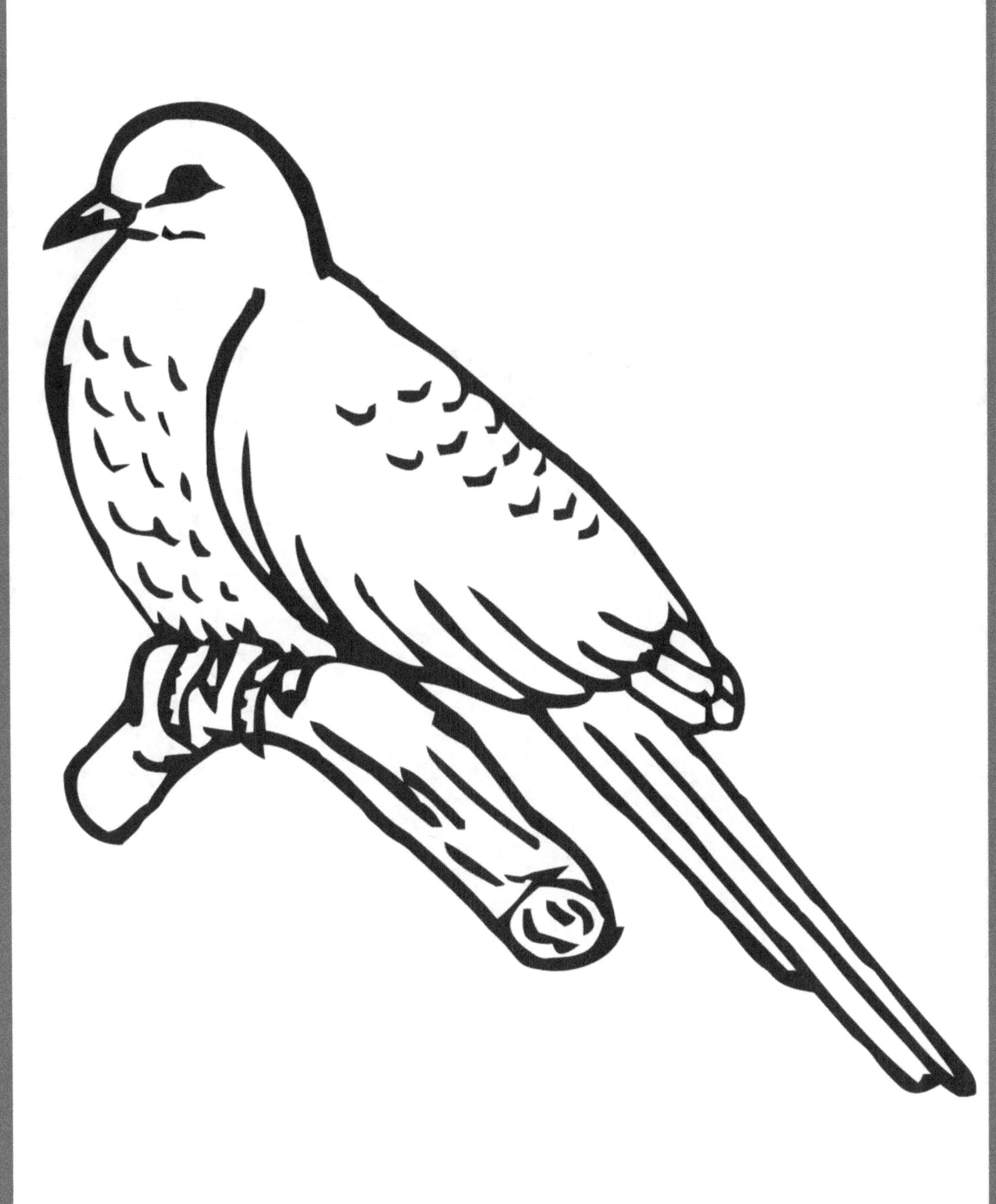

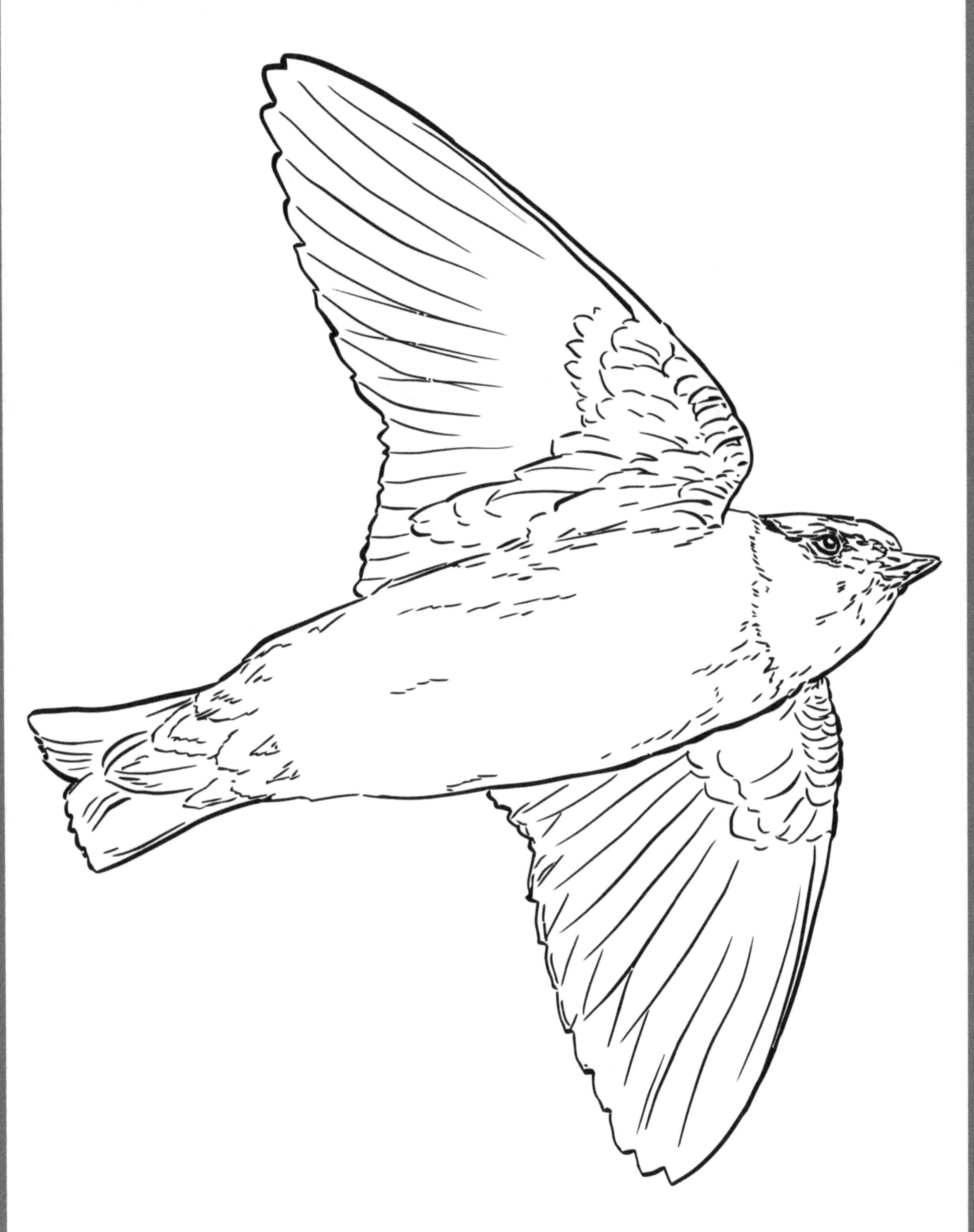

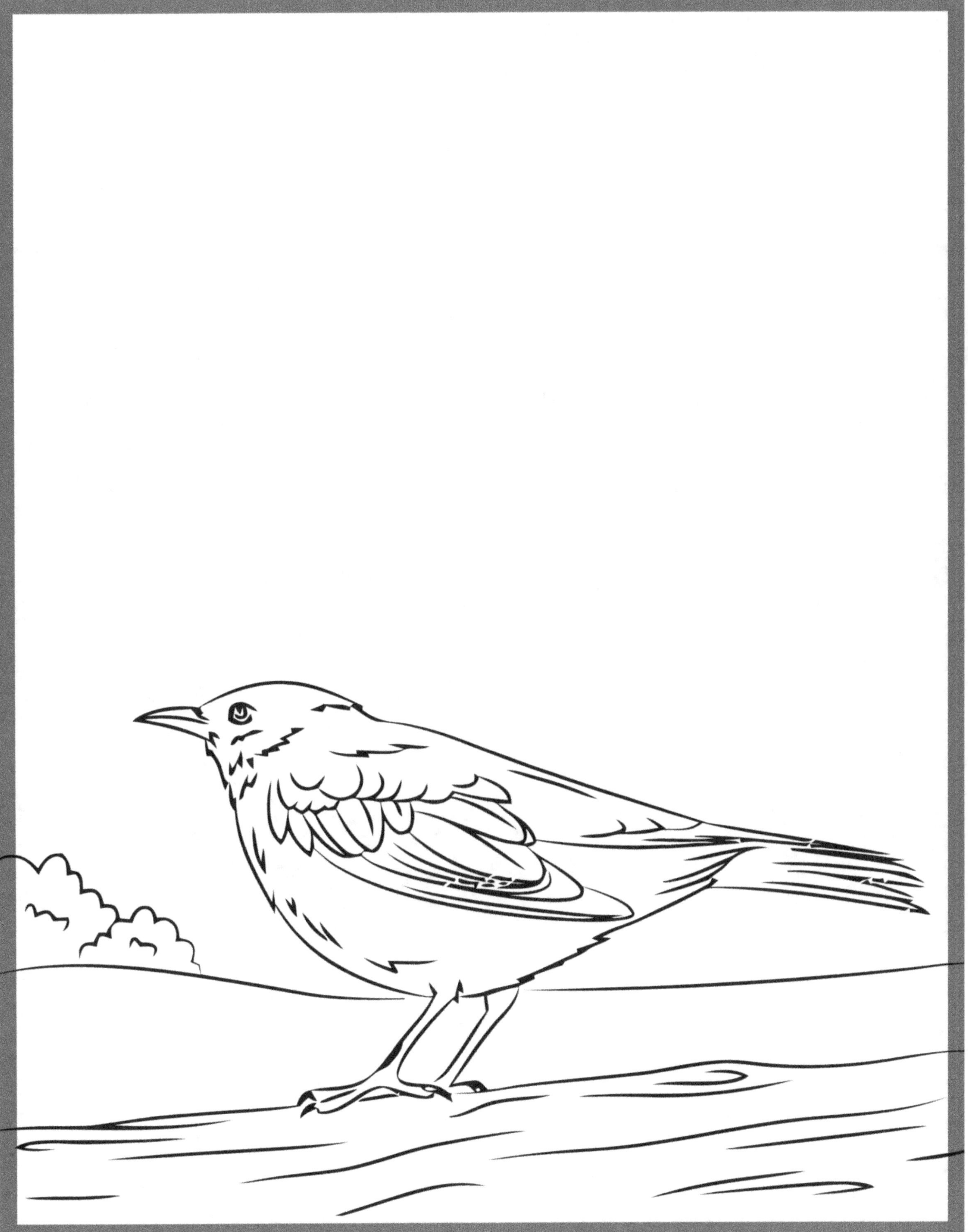

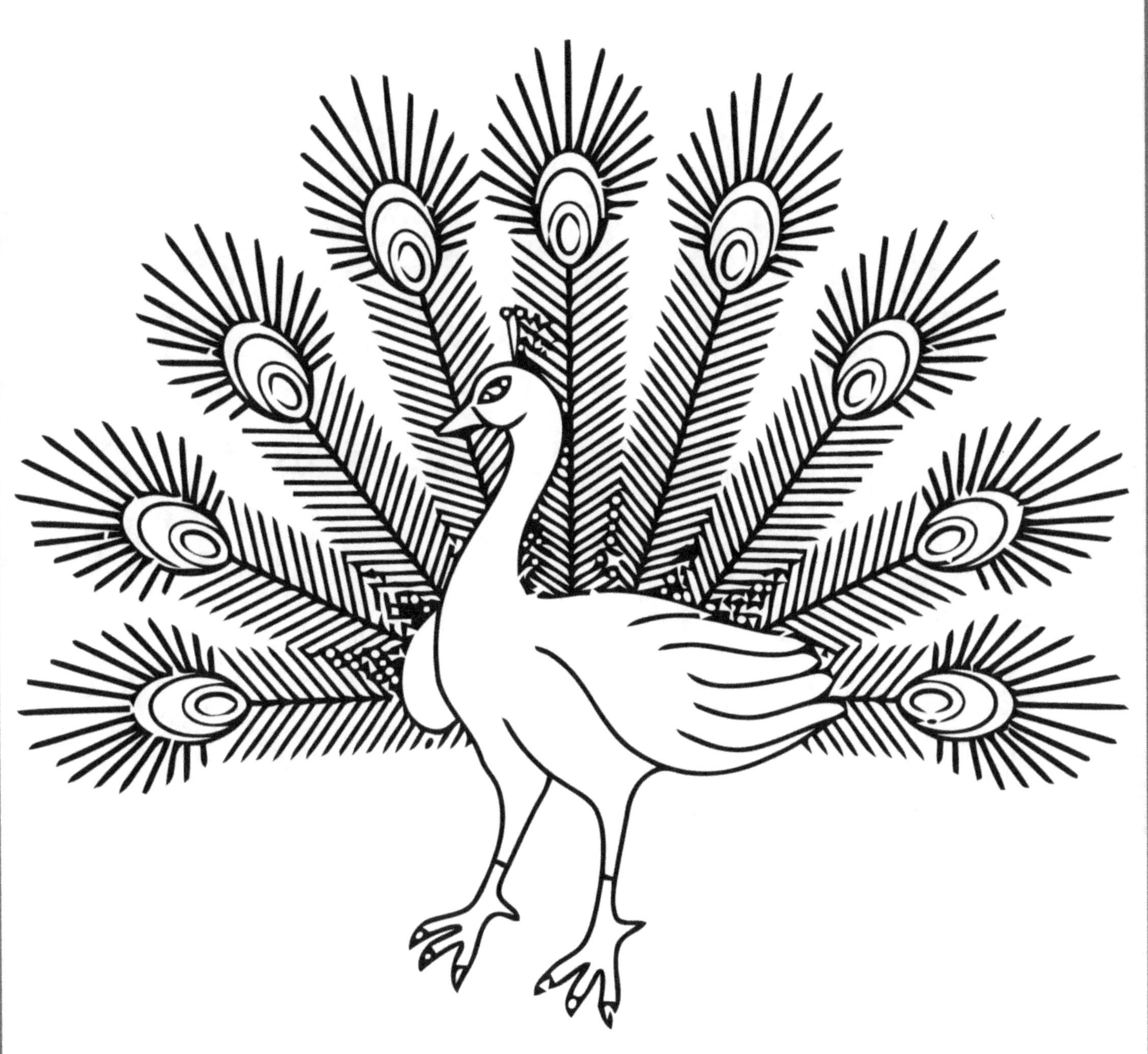

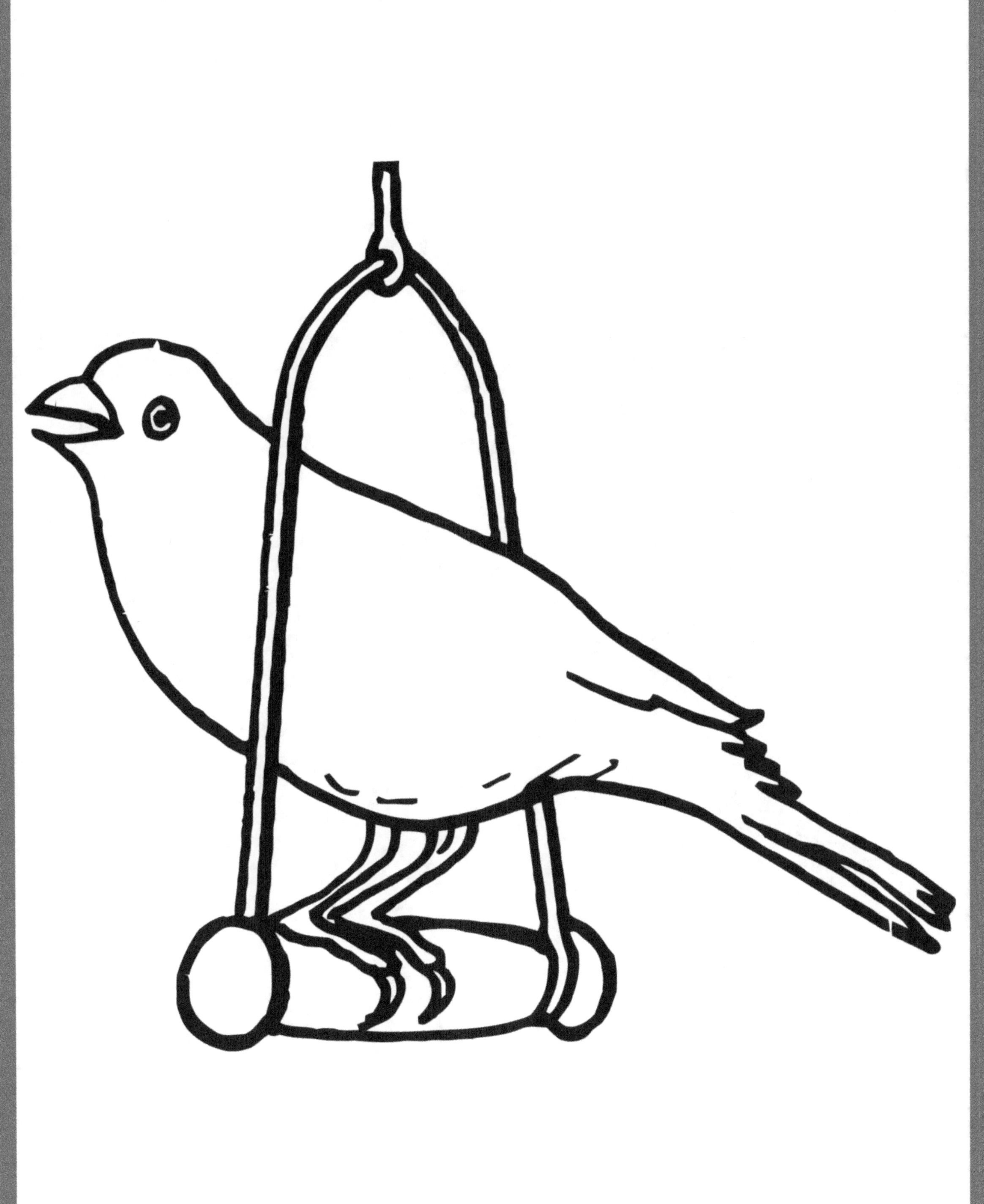

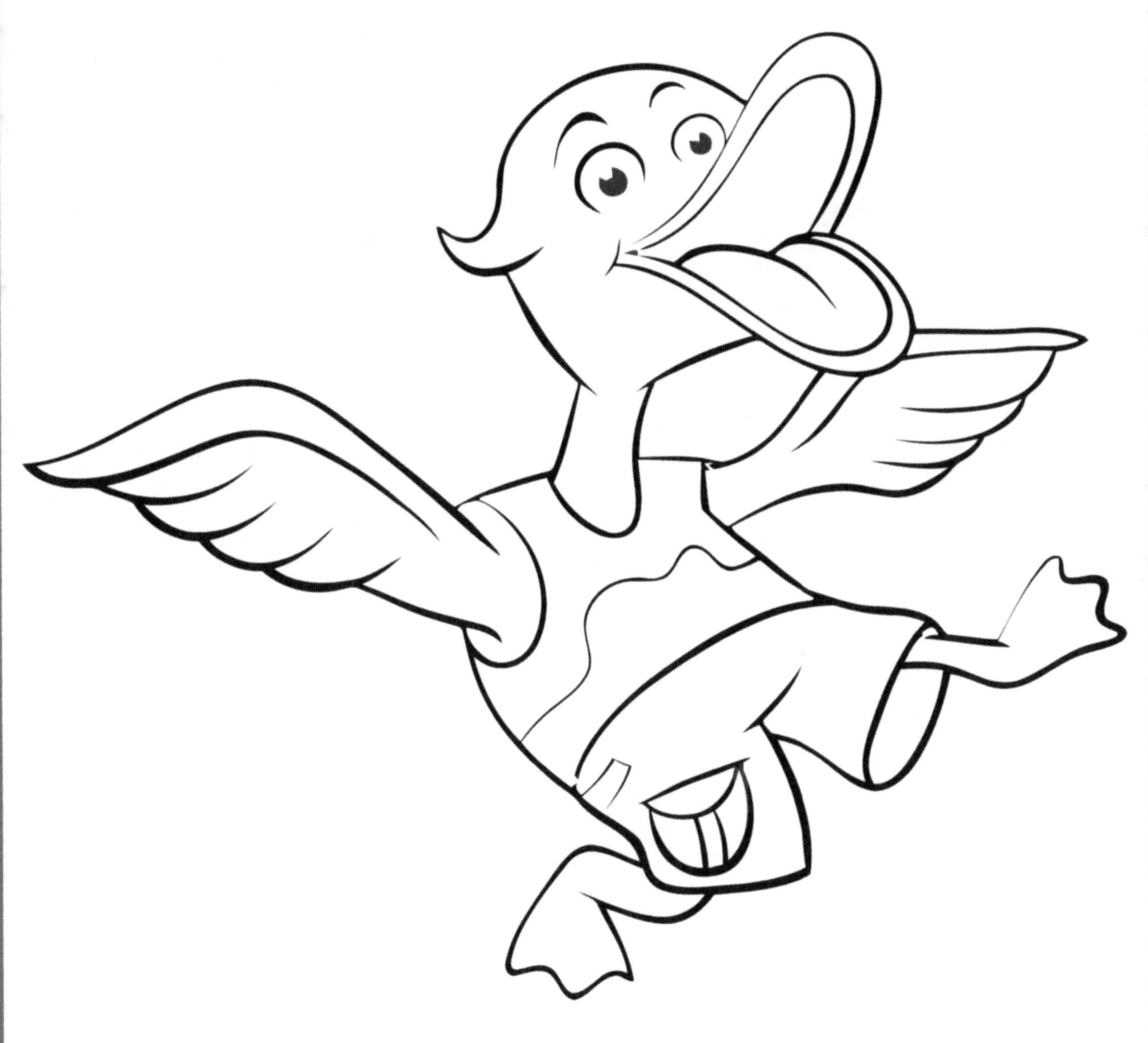

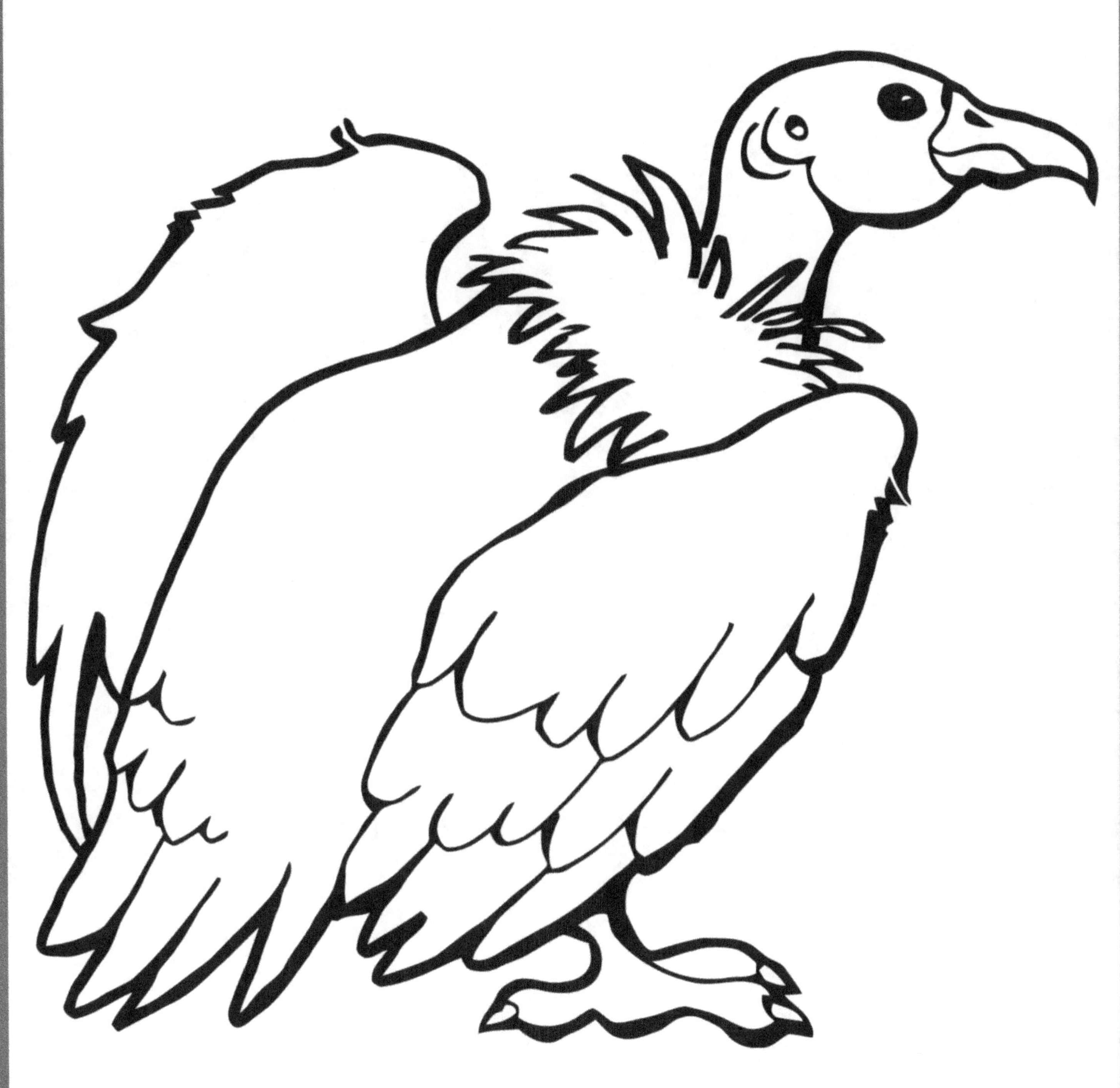

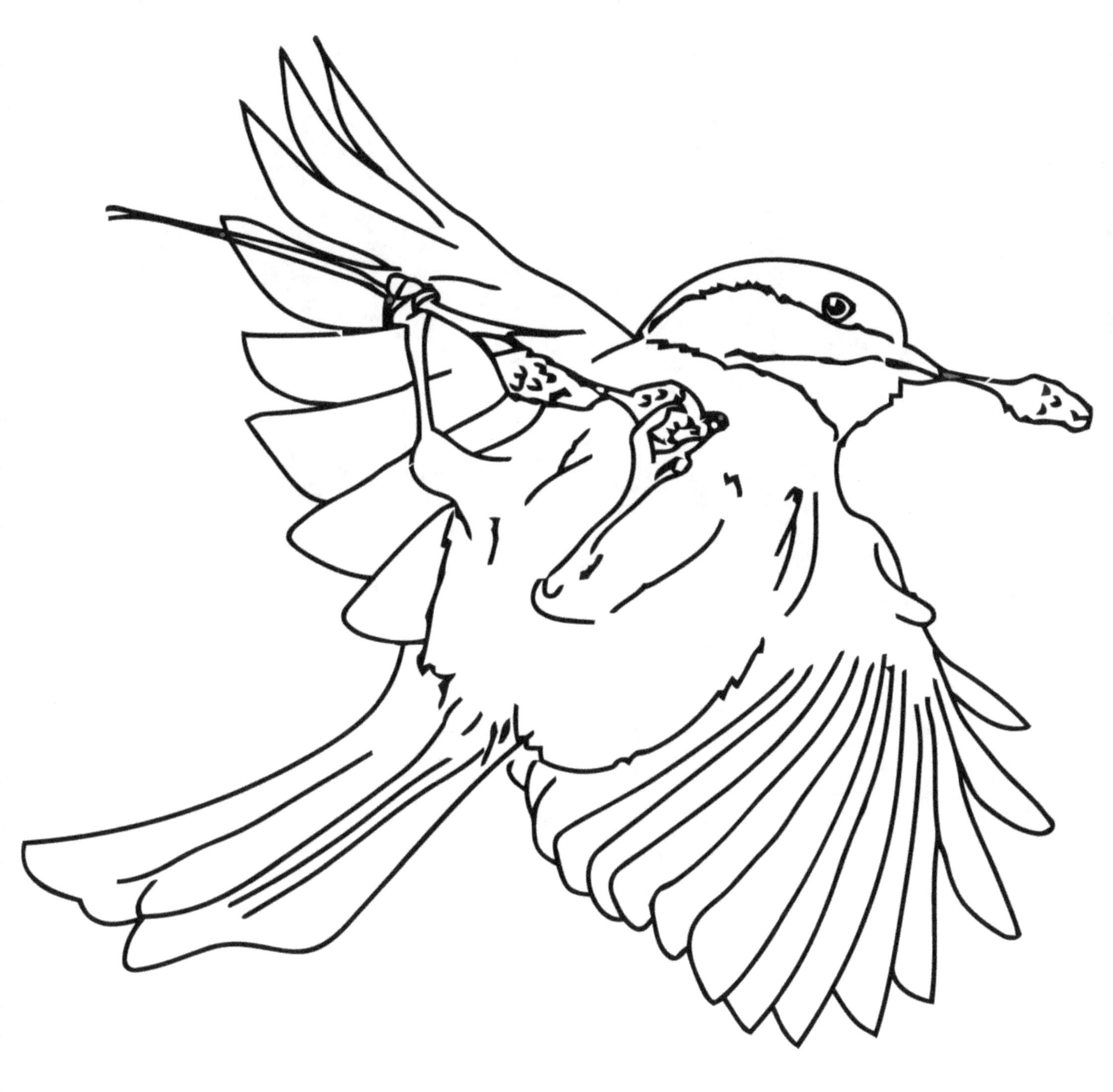